CRAFT GUIDES

Repairing
OLD CHINA
and
CERAMIC
TILES

Jeff Oliver

CHARTWELL
BOOKS. INC

Editor: Anne Yelland
Editorial consultant: Victoria Keller
Art director: Glynis Edwards
Designer: Sylvia Tate
Illustrators: Hussein Hussein, Aziz Khan, Coral Mula, Stuart Perry, Rob Shone
Photography: Jon Bouchier
Studio: Del & Co
Picture research: Liz Eddison

CHARTWELL BOOKS
A division of Book Sales, Inc.
POST OFFICE BOX 7100
114 Northfield Avenue
Edison, N.J. 08818-7100

CLB 4482
© 1995 CLB Publishing, Godalming, Surrey, U.K.
All rights reserved
Printed and bound in Singapore
ISBN 0-7858-0404-8

Contents

Introduction

Due to the very nature of the material, much old china and pottery has suffered damage to some degree, and favourite ceramic items are easily chipped or broken. A missing hand on a figurine, or an ugly discoloured chip on a bowl, detracts greatly from the beauty and integrity of the piece. The effect of even quite a simple restoration can be extremely pleasing and worthwhile.

This book will be of value to those who wish to learn the basic skills of ceramic repair. It will be useful to collectors of antiques, who may have in their collection damaged pieces which they would like to see recover their original beauty, and to the serious student who wishes to learn restoration up to a high standard.

Although every damage is in some way different, all the types of repair you are likely to come across are described in the book as separate projects. The techniques are those used by professional restorers, but they are explained in a way which anyone can follow.

No craft can be rushed; patience will avoid errors, and ultimately produce the most satisfactory results. You cannot expect to finish in one session. Even in the simplest repair, there are various stages necessary for a good result. The piece may need to be left to soak, to dry, or to set for hours, or overnight, before you recommence the work. Have a few broken items to hand, so that as you leave one, you can work on another.

China restoration is not an expensive hobby; indeed, many of the items listed in the tools and materials section can be found in your kitchen or toolbox. The only costly pieces of equipment are an airbrush (spray gun) and compressor, but they are optional. Nor do you need to set up a special workspace, although you may wish to do so. Damaged antique china is easily available, and sometimes remarkably cheap. Sometimes, applying some of the simple techniques, such as stain removing and filling, can increase the value of a piece, or at least make it far more pleasing to the eye.

As with any skilled activity, do not be too ambitious at first. Start with some simple repairs, learning the basic bonding skills on a piece with one or two breaks. Restore a few chips around the edge of a bowl or vase, before embarking on the more complicated tasks of replacing missing parts and more elaborate modelling.

Left: *The basic skills of china repair are not difficult to learn, and applying even some of the simpler techniques can greatly enhance a collection.*

Tools and materials

All the tools and materials you will need to complete the projects in this book should be available from either a hardware or DIY store; an art and/or craft shop; good toy shops, especially those which specialize in models, or specialist model shops; chemists (pharmacists); and, finally, car accessory shops. Department stores with good toy departments are worth investigating.

Art shops are often prepared to order goods in small quantities if they do not stock them, and you should look through their catalogues for various alternatives. Similarly, chemists will usually order goods which they may not have in stock.

As a general rule, buy the smallest quantities available.

The workspace

You need a table (or bench), a chair, a good light, and adequate ventilation. Many of the solvents you will be using are highly flammable – do not smoke and do not have any naked flames in your workroom. A laminate (formica) top is excellent, but if you are using your kitchen table, for instance, cover it with a board, or lay down some newspaper, and cover that with one or two layers of tissue paper taped down on to the table. Throw away the tissue when you have finished and want to use the table for something else.

General

This section includes those materials and tools which have a variety of uses.

An apron, besides keeping your clothes clean, will ensure that if you drop something, it will be caught in your lap.

An eye-dropper is used for transferring drops of acetone, glaze, paint thinners, and so on.

Small clear glass jars with lids are useful for decanting large amounts of filling powders, liquids and so on, for ease of access. Do not use plastic ones which may dissolve in acetone and paint thinners. The more you have the better. Ask for them in your local chemist.

A white tile, preferably several; these are used for mixing fillers and paints.

Petroleum jelly is used as a releasing agent.

A domestic oven or low temperature plate warmer is useful for a variety of jobs, but only vital if you decide to use stoving enamels (pp. 54-5). An electric oven is best. Never heat china to more than 120°C (250°F).

Acetone is the best and most easily available all-round solvent and cleaner for china restoring. You can use it, for example, to clean adhesives before they dry. Paint thinners are alternative solvents.

Soft toilet paper and small cotton rags are used mainly for cleaning-up. Make sure rags are cotton, not man-made fibres, which can dissolve in acetone.

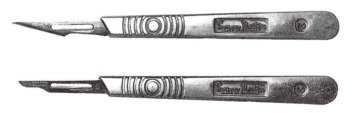

A scalpel (or similar sharp knife) is important and a no 15, with its curved blade, is the most useful. Buy a no 11 next. If, generally, you use more than one type of blade, use a separate handle for each.

Scissors and **tweezers** will also be necessary.

Dismantling

Stipple on water-soluble paint stripper with an old paintbrush to break down old glue.

Water-soluble paint stripper is the best product for breaking down glues, but treat it with caution. If you get any on your skin, wash immediately in cold, not hot, water. *Never* pour hot water on to ceramics covered with paint stripper – noxious fumes are given off.

An old stiff paintbrush is used to apply paint stripper.

Cleaning and stain removal

Washing-up (dishwashing) liquid is the standard cleaning material. With the possible exception of some soft-bodied ceramics (see pp. 70-5), all pieces, including (especially) the joins, should be washed thoroughly in washing-up liquid and warm water. Do this after dismantling (if dismantling is necessary) and before bonding. Be sure to rinse thoroughly after washing.

A toothbrush is especially useful for washing and cleaning joins and difficult, inaccessible places.

A plastic bowl or bucket is a safer container to wash and soak things in than an enamel or metal sink.

Water softener is sold in a powder form. This is *not* the same as fabric softener.

Biological detergent

Hydrogen peroxide 100 volume is used to remove stubborn stains (see pp. 18-19). Make sure you get the full-strength 100 volume. Buy it from the chemist.

Cotton wool (absorbent cotton)

Bonding

Slow-setting epoxy-resin adhesive is the basic and best adhesive for china restoration. It is widely available under various different brand names, but they all consist of two tubes, a *hardener* and a *resin*, which have to be mixed together in equal quantities. Ensure that the two parts are thoroughly mixed together before use. The mixture remains usable for at least an hour, and sets hard after 24 hours, though full strength is achieved only after several days. Slow-setting epoxy resin is also used as the base for filler.

Some people are allergic to epoxy resins, so avoid getting them on your skin.

Fast-setting epoxy resin is not as strong as the slow-setting variety, but it can be useful (see pp. 14-15).

PVA, or wood glue is used for bonding soft-bodied ceramics.

An orange stick or similar tool is used for mixing and applying adhesives and fillers. Orange sticks are available in packets from a chemist. Clean them in acetone before the adhesive dries.

A palette knife is more permanent and versatile, or any small modelling tool with a thin, flexible, metal end can be used. A no 15 scalpel can also be used for applying adhesive.

Thin white card or white cartridge paper is useful for mixing up adhesives on. This can be thrown away after use, which is much easier than cleaning off your white tile. Save the backs of old greeting cards for this purpose.

Razor blade

Filling in and modelling

Slow-setting epoxy resin is used as the base for making up filler (see pp. 8-9 and 30-1).

Ready bought epoxy-resin putties are more convenient to use than home mixed, especially for modelling. They tend to dry a little faster than made-up filler, which is often an advantage. Buy them in craft, modelling or DIY (hardware) shops. See pp. 30-1 for more details.

Titanium dioxide is a strong white pigment, available from art shops.

Kaolin, or fine dental plaster is used to give the filler 'body'. Kaolin powder is probably easier to obtain (from a chemist) than fine dental plaster, although they are equally effective.

Cellulose filler is a more suitable filler for earthenware, terracotta and other soft-bodied ceramics. It is available from hardware or DIY shops, where it is sold as a filler for small holes in walls.

Fine surface filler is used for filling tiny holes. You can buy this in the same range as cellulose filler, or make your own from epoxy resin, titanium dioxide and talcum powder.

Talcum powder can be used with epoxy resins for making up a fine surface filler (see above).

Dividers or callipers are very useful for comparing sizes when you are modelling, as well as measuring distances between repeated painted patterns.

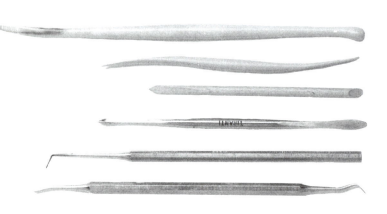

Modelling tools will be necessary. A spatula with a fine, flexible, metal end is probably the most useful all-round tool. A palette knife, small boxwood tools, orange sticks, wooden cocktail sticks, scalpels, dental probes and so on, can all be used.

Rubbing down and abrading

Needle files are available in a variety of shapes. The rounded ones tend to be more useful.

Abrasive papers are essential. The following grades should cover most needs.

Coarse or fairly coarse grade glasspaper is useful but be careful how you use these papers, as they can scratch the glaze on the original china if you are careless. Medium grade glasspaper is probably the most useful. Flour paper is a fine abrasive paper for finishing.

Silicon carbide wet and dry paper (grade 1200) is available from car-accessory shops, and used for very fine smoothing, especially between coats of paint and varnish.

Moulds

Liquid rubber latex is usually sold as fabric adhesive, and is a good, easily available material from which to make moulds (see pp. 44-7).

Fine sawdust is used for strengthening moulds.

Cotton-wool buds (Q-tip swabs) are useful for applying latex to a model.

A palette knife or small metal spatula, orange sticks and a scalpel are the basic modelling tools you will need. They should be either metal or wooden – not plastic, which can dissolve in some solvents.

Painting and colouring

Artist's dry fine-ground pigments are very strong, so buy the smallest quantities you can. They are often sold in small glass tubes. A list of the colours you will need is given on pp. 52-3. These are *not* the same as the school-type powder paints.

Ready-made paints are a convenient alternative to dry pigments, or you can invest in both. The most common available series are those sold for painting model aircraft, but you might find a specialist set for china restoring or glass painting in a good art or craft shop.

Glazes or varnish mediums are discussed on pp. 54-5.

Thinning agents or thinners are used for thinning glazes, varnishes and paints, and may be used instead of acetone for cleaning.

Metal dippers from art and craft shops are useful for mixing paints in.

A black tile is good for practising white and background painting.

An old, fairly soft brush (about a size 6) can be used for mixing paints on your tile or in a metal dipper.

Best-quality sable brushes should be used for painting. Cheaper brushes do not last as long, and will soon start to leave hairs on your work. Look after them, they are both delicate and expensive. To begin with, a no 00, for fine decoration, and a no 2 are the most useful.

A hard lead pencil is useful for lightly pencilling in complicated patterns.

Talcum powder can be added to paints and glaze for a matt effect. Pumice, or abrasive powder will give a coarser, gritty effect.

Gilding and lustres

Ready-made gold paints, as well as silver and copper, are available from art shops.

Bronze powders are an alternative to ready-made. They tend to give a slightly better finish, and are more versatile. You can also buy silver and copper powders.

A soft cloth can be used for burnishing.

Ready-made gold paints and bronze powders are generally more appropriate on oriental gold; use transfer gold leaf for a brighter finish.

Gold- and silver-leafing materials

Transfer gold leaf is discussed on pp. 68-9.

Imitation transfer gold leaf is much cheaper than real gold leaf, and on many jobs is just as good, if not better.

Silver leaf is applied in the same way as gold leaf, but tarnishes quite quickly, unless you cover it with a coat of varnish.

Agate burnisher

For advanced painting

The airbrush is discussed in full on pp. 66-7.

A compressor feeds compressed air to the airbrush.

A vapour mask should be used with an airbrush.

Masking tape is useful to avoid spraying larger areas than you need. The type that peels off easily is the best.

Supporting

Before you begin any bonding job, you must consider how the item is to be supported and strapped together. Clear adhesive tape and tourniquets can be used to strap tight and secure simple breaks together while the adhesive cures. But these are not appropriate when you are bonding small or awkward pieces on an ornamental figure, for instance.

Many amateurs attempt to overcome the problem by using fast-setting glues, the most extreme being the 'superglues' (cyanoacrylates) which set in under a minute. These are not suitable for use on china. For one thing, mistakes cannot be rectified without going through the tedious business of dismantling the join (see pp. 22-3) and starting again. With slow-setting epoxy resin, you have the time necessary to achieve the most perfect join. In addition, no available adhesive has the strength of a slow-setting epoxy resin.

Always position the piece you are working on in such a manner as to maximize the effect of gravity.

Support an arm with modelling clay, and use a core of it in a spout as a support when filling.

Support bonded plates and cup handles in a sandbox at an angle to maximize the effect of gravity.

A tourniquet is the best way to hold the two sides of a simple crack or break firm while the glue dries. An old pair of tights makes an ideal tourniquet. Tie them round the vase or plate with a loose knot, then insert a stick in the knot and twist the stick until the tourniquet is tight.

Clear adhesive tape (Sellotape/scotch tape) is useful for holding both sides of a break together while slow-setting epoxy resin dries. If it leaves a sticky residue on the surface, clean it off with acetone. Do not use this tape on gilding – it can lift gilding off.

Stationery clips (bull-dog clips) are useful for holding the sides of a join in a plate or saucer in perfect alignment.

A sandbox or a tin full of sand or salt is a valuable aid for positioning pieces of ceramics at whatever angle is most appropriate. Use a cake tin or a box – a cat-litter tray is an ideal size.

Plastic modelling clay (plasticine) is almost indispensable for propping up and supporting in position. It becomes soft and pliable when warm, yet maintains its shape well, and can be removed easily. Do not allow it to come into contact with the join.

Fast-setting epoxy resin can be used if you can find no effective means of support. This is not as strong as slow-setting, but on many small pieces, great strength is not of crucial importance.

Mix up the fast-setting resin in the same way as you would the slow-setting type, and apply it thinly to one side of the join. Make sure you have practised joining the broken piece without adhesive to familiarize yourself with the join, and the best way of holding it together with your fingers.

Fast-setting epoxy resin takes 10-15 minutes to harden, so after mixing, leave it for five minutes, then press the broken piece on to the join and hold it there for between five and ten minutes more until the adhesive has hardened. Use a firm even pressure. Do remember, however, that holding something for five or ten minutes without moving is not easy.

Whatever method of support you choose, check its effectiveness after two hours. Make sure none of the pieces have moved, and if one (or more) has, then readjust it.

Project 1: Cracked oriental vase

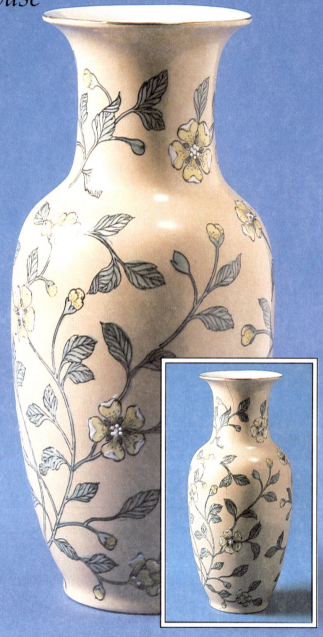

This vase, with its long vertical crack, is in danger of splitting in two, and the crack is so visible because of its accumulation of dirt and grease. The first step is to draw out all the dirt. For this you will need biological detergent and water softener, but if this method fails, you may need hydrogen peroxide 100 volume. Slow-setting epoxy-resin adhesive is used to bond the crack. When heated, this adhesive turns liquid, before setting rock hard. If you first warm the vase, the epoxy resin will seep right into the crack.

A tourniquet ensures a tight, neat join while the adhesive dries, by exerting a strong pressure in one direction. Sometimes this is not appropriate or possible, in which case use clear adhesive tape to strap the join as tightly as you can.

If you have a piece of china with an unsightly hairline crack, use the stain removing techniques alone. It is not necessary to fill in the crack, because the piece is unlikely to be in any danger of splitting.

A near invisible repair can be made using these techniques.

Left and above: *On a crack such as this, the secret of a really invisible repair is to ensure that all the dirt and grime are removed before the crack is secured with slow-setting epoxy-resin adhesive.*

To remove dirt and staining

Mix up in a plastic bucket a weak solution of equal quantities of water softener and biological detergent. Add warm water to a level which will enable you to submerge the vase completely. Do not use very hot water as this reduces the effectiveness of the cleaning solution. Leave the vase in the solution for several hours or overnight. If the crack is still dirty, scrub at it with an old toothbrush, then repeat the soaking in a new cleaning solution. Repeat as often as necessary.

If the soaking method does not completely remove every particle of dirt, try pouring a small quantity of hydrogen peroxide 100 volume on to a saucer. *Be careful* not to touch this with your fingers as it is corrosive. With some tweezers, soak a swab of cotton wool in the peroxide, and place the swab along the crack – you might need several swabs depending on the size of the crack. Leave these for several hours, then remove them. The hydrogen peroxide will cause the dirt to leach out into the cotton wool. Repeat the process if necessary.

Do not use peroxide on soft pottery or earthenware; it can cause the stain to spread.

Rinse the vase thoroughly in clean water, and leave it to dry in a warm place.

Securing the crack

Gently warm the vase in an oven at its lowest setting for about 10 minutes, or use a hair dryer to heat the crack. While the vase is warming, mix up some *slow-setting* epoxy resin on a square of white card. Use an orange stick or palette knife to mix the two parts together.

Remove the vase from the oven – use a tea towel (pot holder), it might be hotter than you think. Insert a razor blade in the crack, and carefully open the crack a fraction. Apply the adhesive liberally to the crack – because of the heat, the adhesive will immediately seep into it. Remove the razor blade. If there is a good deal of adhesive around the cracked area, carefully remove it with acetone or a similar solvent, but do not allow the solvent to touch the crack itself. Any remaining adhesive around the crack can be removed later.

Tighten the two sides of the crack together using a tourniquet and leave it for at least 12 hours. Remove the tourniquet and pare off any excess dried adhesive with a scalpel or a similar sharp knife.

Cleaning and repairing a crack

1 Soak vase in water softener and detergent.

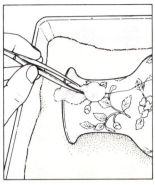

2 Lay cotton wool swabs along the crack.

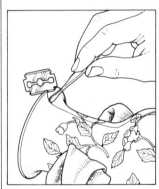

3 Open crack a fraction and apply the glue.

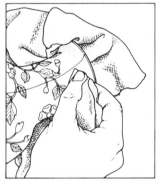

4 Clean off excess adhesive with acetone.

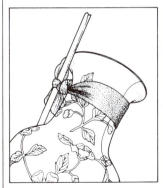

5 Use a tourniquet to ensure a clean join.

6 Pare off excess dried adhesive with a scalpel.

Project 2: Broken plate

Simple breaks

Technique, in an apparently simple job, can make the difference between an amateurish, weak join, and a near invisible professional repair.

The plate illustrated had been badly glued together. The old glue was applied too thickly, and had in time turned a lumpy, dirty brown. The first task was to dismantle the original repair, then clean off every trace of the old glue before rebonding the pieces.

For dismantling, you will need hot water and a plastic bowl. It may seem surprising, but with prolonged immersion in water alone, most glues will soften and break. If soaking alone does not work, you will need water-soluble paint stripper and, possibly, acetone. Water-soluble paint stripper will not damage the ceramic or glaze, but it will dissolve old restored materials and, occasionally, old gilding. If your plate has gilding, be a little wary and test a tiny part first.

Slow-setting epoxy resin is used for bonding. While the adhesive is drying, the two parts of the plate need to be held together as tightly as possible. Clear adhesive tape and a tourniquet are used for this, although you may also need metal stationery (bull-dog) clips to hold the two sides of the break in good alignment.

One of the interesting things about china restoration is that no two repairs are exactly the same. However, the same basic techniques apply whether the mend is simple or complex. They are not difficult, but forethought and planning are essential. Do not embark upon one step before you are sure of the next, and have all the appropriate materials to hand.

This book is intended to show you how to repair ornamental china and ceramics. Domestic china, especially plates, can only rarely be satisfactorily repaired. All adhesives will eventually break down in water, especially in a dishwasher, and, of course, on a broken plate, dirt and grime will soon start to accumulate in the crack, however perfectly you have joined the two halves. It is worth repairing the broken handle on your favourite cup, or one of a set, if you bond and strap it properly. But be careful when you wash it, and use it as little as possible.

Left: *The combination of adhesive tape and a tourniquet, as well as the use of a minimum amount of adhesive, enables you to make a really tight, neat and secure join on a two-piece break.*

Dismantling the old join

Place the plate in a plastic bowl, pour in enough very hot water to cover it and leave it to soak for a few hours or overnight. Repeat every few hours as necessary.

If, after a few days, the join refuses to come apart, take it out of the water and dry it off. Stipple water-soluble paint stripper on to both sides of the join, leave it for about 20 minutes, then wipe off the stripper. If the join is really stubborn, stipple on the stripper, then enclose the plate in a plastic bag; this will stop the paint stripper drying out and give it more time to work.

It is not uncommon to find a broken plate or bowl which has been riveted together with metal staples, held in place with plaster. To remove these, soak the piece in warm water for a few hours. This should dissolve most of the plaster, making it fairly easy to lever out the staples with a scalpel. Start from the middle one and work outwards to the edges.

A certain amount of old glue will probably still adhere to each side of the now-broken join. Apply paint

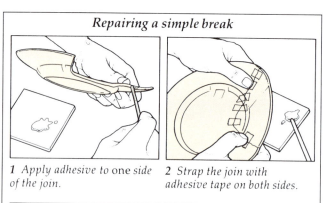

Repairing a simple break

1 *Apply adhesive to one side of the join.*

2 *Strap the join with adhesive tape on both sides.*

3 *Use a tourniquet to maintain firm pressure.*

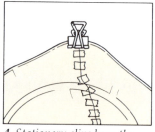

4 *Stationery clips keep the rim well aligned.*

stripper to each edge, leave it for 20 minutes, then carefully remove the stripper and dissolved glue with a scalpel. Be careful not to damage the broken edges of the plate with your scalpel. Repeat this process if necessary. If the old glue has stained the joined edges, use the methods outlined on pp. 18-19 to remove the staining before you proceed.

Clean the plate thoroughly with a toothbrush and washing-up (dishwashing) liquid. Rinse it in clean water and leave until it is bone dry.

Dry run

Before you start applying any adhesive, always work out how the pieces fit together. *This is a must for every bonding job.* If you find your join is not perfect, examine it carefully under a good light or a magnifying glass, to check for minute deposits of glue, or tiny shards of china. Carefully remove these with your scalpel, not your fingers. Position the broken pieces together several times, so you are familiar with their alignment.

Bonding and strapping

On some white card, thoroughly mix up a small quantity of slow-setting epoxy resin with an orange stick or similar tool. The adhesive will remain workable for at least an hour, so do not hurry these stages.

Cut up about a dozen strips of clear adhesive tape, and make sure they are easily to hand.

With your orange stick, carefully apply the epoxy resin to one side of the join only, making sure that you do not miss any area. Contrary to what you might think, the thinner the layer of adhesive, the stronger and closer the bond.

Press the two pieces of china together. Be firm but gentle, or you might chip off tiny pieces of ceramic in the join, which will cause it to misalign. Test the alignment by running a scalpel across it from side to side; it will catch where one side is higher than the other. Adjust as necessary. While maintaining the pressure, strap the join with pieces of clear adhesive tape on both sides of the plate.

Support the join as shown opposite. After 24 hours, remove the clips, tourniquet and adhesive tape and pare off any excess adhesive with a scalpel. If the tape has left a sticky residue, clean it off with acetone.

Project 3: Porcelain saucer

The problem of multiple breaks

The difference between this and the previous project is, of course, its complexity. This porcelain saucer was broken into 14 pieces. Fortunately, none of the pieces were lost, and, since fine porcelain is a glass-like material, it does not flake or chip easily, so you will not have to make up any new pieces. Nonetheless, this is a fairly extreme example of a multiple break, and, when you first start, you should try something in fewer pieces than this. If you have had plenty of practice on simpler multiple breaks of three, four or five pieces, you will feel confident enough to tackle something of this complexity. The method is the same. You may have to dismantle old joins, but even if you do not, you must clean everything thoroughly before you proceed. You should work out how the pieces fit together, and do a 'dry run', that is, position all pieces as you would if you were gluing the item, but without glue. This is so that when you apply the glue, you know exactly how the pieces fit together. Finally, the piece is bonded and strapped, and the joins checked after an hour or two to ensure that they have not moved.

On multiple breaks, much more time should be spent on the dry run than on a simple break, so that there is no doubt in your mind where every piece goes, and the order in which they should be joined.

You will only need those materials used in project 2, plus pencil and paper.

Do not be tempted to paint fine porcelain like this saucer. Because the ceramic is so thin, light shines through it and, if you hold it up to the light, any painting will show as a thick, fuzzy, dark line.

Cleaning

With a toothbrush, wash the pieces carefully in a plastic bowl partly filled with warm water and washing-up (dishwashing) liquid. Rinse them thoroughly, then put them somewhere warm to dry. When they are dry, examine the edges to check that they are perfectly clean. If not, use the stain removing techniques described on pp. 18-19.

Left: *It is best to join multiple breaks in one session, so allow yourself plenty of time and make sure that everything is to hand and that you have cut up enough strips of adhesive tape.*

Planning the reconstruction

Before you start thinking about bonding, lay out all the pieces on a spotlessly clean board or table surface, and study them carefully to see how they fit together. When you have worked out the jigsaw of pieces, sketch it out on a piece of paper for reference. Try not to handle any edges, as deposits of grease can weaken and discolour the join.

You then have to decide the *order* of bonding. If you bond pieces together at random, you will almost certainly be left at the end with one or more pieces which do not make a proper fit (this is called 'locking out'). If you are in any doubt, especially with a complicated project such as this one, first tape everything together in a dry run. If you find one or more pieces that do not fit properly, try them in a different order until they do. Number the pieces on your sketch, so that you can refer to it as you work.

Preparation for bonding

Use slow-setting epoxy resin for bonding. Before you start, cut up plenty of strips of clear adhesive tape of various sizes, including some very small ones, and arrange them along the edge of a table. Do not wait until you have started bonding, as this stage is delicate and tricky: everything must be at hand.

Bonding and strapping

Apply the adhesive to all the pieces as described on pp. 22-3. It is even more important with multiple breaks to cover only one side of the join with adhesive, and in as thin a layer as possible. Remember that each layer of adhesive adds more material to the saucer, and, with many joins, increases the problem of locking out.

Refer to your sketch and press together pieces 1 and 2. If some epoxy resin is squeezed out it means that you have not applied it thinly enough. Before the adhesive sets, it can be wiped off with acetone on a clean cotton rag – do not use a paper tissue (Kleenex) which will leave traces of paper on your join. While you are pressing the two pieces together, strap the join with clear adhesive tape on both sides and check the alignment with your scalpel (see p. 23). When you are

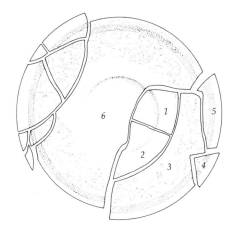

Sketch, and number, the pieces in order of bonding to avoid the problem of locking out.

Patience and forethought, rather than great skill, produce good results on a complicated multiple break like this one.

satisfied, press pieces 1 and 2, to piece 3, and repeat the checking and strapping. Carry on doing this until the saucer is complete. If any pieces have moved, you will have time to make careful adjustments.

After a couple of hours, check that no join has moved. If one (or more) has, and you cannot adjust it, break down all the joins with paint stripper (see pp. 22-3) and start again – it is far easier to do this at this stage than after the glue has set hard.

After 24 hours, remove the adhesive tape and clean off the excess adhesive as described on p. 23.

Project 4: Chipped vase

The use of coloured filler

This project demonstrates how to fill in chips and make up simple missing parts. There are two ways of colouring a filled-in piece: you can either use coloured filler, or paint. Painting is a more complicated procedure and is dealt with in full on pp. 48-59. Here, we will use coloured filler, which is simpler, but more approximate in matching colours than painting. It can give good results, however, especially when the piece to be filled is a uniform colour.

If your piece has an intricate design, you can use coloured filler for the background colour, and paint the decoration on top, or use plain white filler and paint it all (see pp. 56-7).

Even if you decide eventually to paint, follow the instructions for making filler and filling in chips and breaks which are outlined here.

Materials

To make the filler you will need some slow-setting epoxy resin, a selection of dry artist's pigments (the colours you may need are discussed in more detail on pp. 52-3), some kaolin or fine dental plaster, and, possibly, a fine surface filler. Mix up your filler and colours on a plain white tile. Have several to hand if possible – they are very useful – and keep a small bowl of water and some acetone handy.

An alternative to making up your own filler is to use one of the ready-made epoxy-resin putties on the market. If you buy an opaque type, you will also need some titanium dioxide to whiten it. These putties can also be coloured with artist's pigments.

Any small modelling tools you can find are helpful, in particular a small metal spatula. For rubbing down, small metal files are useful, but the various grades of glasspaper are a must. If you want a glass-like finish, use one of the glazes discussed on pp. 54-5. You may also need clear adhesive tape and plastic modelling clay for support.

Left: *The edges of plates, cups and as here, vases, are the parts most prone to chipping. There are two basic types of chips – glaze chips and V-shaped chips. Repairs to a V chip like this one are more time-consuming because you have to model on both the inside and the outside of the piece.*

Making epoxy-resin filler

Make up some slow-setting epoxy resin on a piece of white card as described on p. 18. When it is thoroughly mixed, transfer some to a clean white tile.

Look at the vase and study its colour. Select the dry fine-ground artist's pigments that you think are the nearest to the ones you need. Carefully decant tiny piles of each pigment on to another tile, but keep them well away from each other. Many pieces of china have a predominantly near white background colour, so you will probably need some titanium dioxide which is a strong white powder pigment. If this is the case, mix it in first.

Carefully add grains of the appropriate pigment(s) to the mixed epoxy resin (a scalpel is useful for transferring pigments), and mix it up with your orange stick until you have a uniform colour. These pigments vary in strength, but many are very strong indeed, so be cautious and introduce just a few grains at a time (for hints on colour matching, see pp. 56-9).

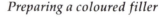

Preparing a coloured filler

1 Make up some slow-setting epoxy resin.

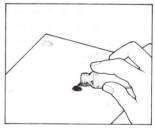

2 Decant piles of powder pigments to a clean tile.

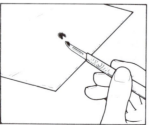

3 Transfer pigments to resin with a scalpel.

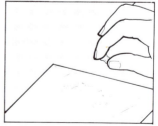

4 Add filling powder until the filler is stiff.

Have some acetone and a cotton rag handy to clean epoxy resin off your tools and so on, but remember that it will not work on dried epoxy resin.

When the colour is to your satisfaction, you will need to add 'body' to the epoxy resin so it will maintain its shape while it is setting. There are several filling powders you can use, but the two most readily available are kaolin and fine dental plaster. The more filling powder you add, the thicker your putty will become. If you want to fill in small holes or cracks, then the mixture can be kept quite thin, with only a small addition of filling powder, and spread on to the crack or small hole with a fine modelling tool or orange stick. If the chip is more substantial, keep adding filler until you can pick it up in your fingers ('flouring' your fingers with the filler powder helps). Keep adding filler until it is really stiff, so that when you incorporate it on to the missing area, it will keep its shape.

Keep a little filler on a piece of white card, so that if you do need more, you can match up the next batch to the first. If the match is not good, the slightly different shades will give a 'blotchy' look.

Ready-made putties

There are a number of ready-made epoxy-resin putties on the market. These are convenient and save time; they are also easy to work with and hold their shape well. In addition, many do not dry as hard as the made-up filler; this makes them easier to rub down. The only disadvantage is that when they are mixed, some of them have a green, blue or grey colour. There are some which are white or opaque, so buy these for preference.

Tools for filling

The method of filling and the tools you will need depend on the type of chip or missing parts to be filled in. Fingers, scalpels, small metal spatulas and fine modelling tools can all be used, but don't feel you have to invest in a vast range of them. Your fingers, an orange stick and perhaps a small metal spatula or even the blade of a scalpel will do for most jobs. Other tools are useful, but you can buy (or make) them as you see the need, and experience has shown you what might be useful.

Filling

As carefully as possible put a layer of filler in the chip. If the area to be filled is large, do not try to fill all of it at once, as it is bound to sag as it dries. Instead, build up the filling in layers, leaving each layer to dry, or at least partially dry, before adding the next. Try not to overfill the chip more than a fraction. If you do, when the filler dries, you will have to spend many tiresome hours rubbing it down with files and abrasive papers until it is flush with the unbroken edge. If you are in doubt, underfill it, and add more later.

Remember that you are always working in three dimensions, and that you must take into account the curve of the lip of the vase. Water is useful to smooth the filling into shape, as is acetone, but be careful: too much acetone on your modelling tool will temporarily turn your filler into a liquid 'sludge' until the acetone evaporates. Use filling powder on your fingers to 'pat' the filler into shape without it sticking to them.

On a small missing piece, you can save a lot of time by using clear adhesive tape as a backing to press the epoxy-resin putty against. This can be easily removed when the filler has dried. On larger areas, use plastic modelling clay in the same way, but be careful not to allow it to touch the broken edges of the china.

Drying

The filler is ready to be sanded down when it is hard enough to be rubbed by abrasive papers without it peeling off in lumps – usually between six and ten hours, depending on room temperature. However, this 'curing' process can be speeded up by placing the piece in a warm environment such as an airing cupboard (linen closet). If you put the object in an oven at the lowest possible temperature, the filling will harden in about 20 minutes. But beware: if you do cure it in an oven, although you can proceed more quickly, the filler will be very hard indeed and, consequently, much tougher to rub down.

A further word of warning if you are using an oven to speed-cure your filler – leave it to part dry naturally for about two hours before you put it in the oven. If you put it in immediately, the epoxy resin in the filler liquefies with heat and then hardens, so your filler will lose its shape. (See also stoving enamels, pp. 54-5.)

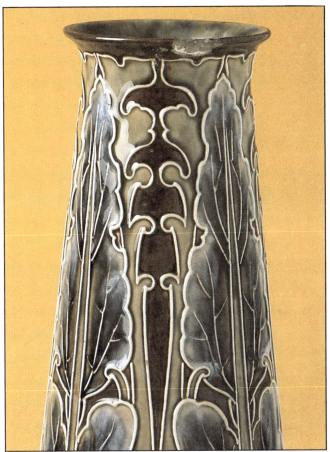

While this glaze chip is obviously simpler to restore than the V-type chip on the gilded vase, it involves filling in and rubbing down on a curved area, which is always more difficult than on a flat surface.

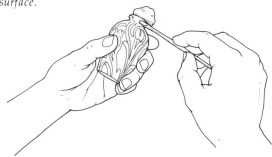

Use a wodge of plastic modelling clay as a backing to build up your filler against.

Rubbing down

When the filler is dry, it will probably need rubbing down with abrasive papers. You can buy small metal files of various shapes to rub away excess filler and you should start with these if you have grossly overfilled. Be very careful not to touch the original glaze on the vase (this is easy to do), which will scratch and damage.

Next, use glasspaper, cut up into 25mm (1in.) squares to finish the rubbing down. Start with a fairly coarse grade, then a medium (the most useful) and finish off with the finest grade you can buy (often called flour paper). This will give you a smooth finish, which can be further improved by rubbing in a fine abrasive metal

Abrading and finishing

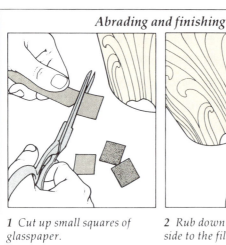

1 Cut up small squares of glasspaper.

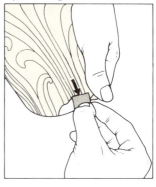

2 Rub down from the china side to the filler.

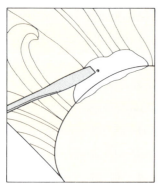

3 Fill in tiny holes with a fine surface filler.

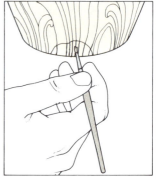

4 Apply a coat of glaze medium.

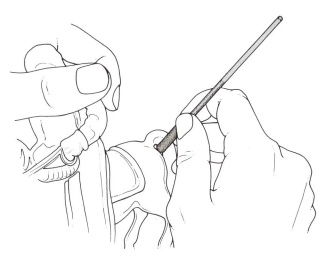

For rubbing down awkward areas, wrap a square of glasspaper around a thin stick or round needle file.

polish paste. As you rub down, be constantly aware of the contours of the shape you are trying to achieve.

As a rule, rub down from the china side to the filler in separate strokes, not the other way round. If you rub down the other way, or you rub along the join with the china rather than across it, you will inevitably rub too much off and will have to fill in around the edge again with new filler. For rubbing down awkward areas, wrap a square of abrasive paper around the end of a small round stick or round needle file.

Filling in

You may need to make up more filler several times, rubbing down between each layer, until your final rubbing down is satisfactory. Tiny holes in your filler can, at this stage, be carefully filled with epoxy resin, or a fine surface filler (see p. 10), both coloured to match.

Finishing

When you have finished all your filling in and rubbing down, examine the surrounding china and clean off any filler that has stuck to it with a scalpel.

If you require a glaze-like finish, paint on a thin coat of varnish (see pp. 54-5).

Project 5: Advanced modelling

Do not be put off by the thought of modelling – you do not have to be the world's greatest modeller to achieve excellent results. What you need are good observation, an eye for fine detail, and patience.

Apart from chips (see pp. 28-35), hands, handles and flowers are probably the commonest parts which need to be replaced on ceramic ornaments and figures. The techniques outlined here can be adapted for just about any other kind of piece you are likely to encounter.

You have one great advantage when you are modelling. If you need to make a hand, you can copy the style, size and colour from the other hand on the figure. On a decorated ornament, an intact flower will be your model for a new one. A missing cup handle has a twin somewhere. If you don't have it, do some research. There are plenty of books illustrating different styles of cup handles (and, for that matter, figurines). Use your library, investigate museums. If you intend to repair more than one or two pieces of china, paste pictures from old antiques magazines into a scrapbook for future reference.

Materials and tools

Epoxy-resin putty (either home-made or ready-bought, which can be easier to model with, see pp. 30-1) can be used for all kinds of intricate modelling. To model fine details, make sure the epoxy build-up is really thick by adding plenty of filling powder. If you intend to paint, add a little titanium dioxide to give you a white base colour. If you wish to use the coloured filler method (see pp. 28-35), add the appropriate pigments.

Do not begin modelling immediately, because the material is initially too soft to support its shape when you are making something as delicate as fingers or a complicated flower. Leave the filler for about two hours, depending on room temperature, by which time it will have started to harden; you will still have at least an hour before it becomes too hard to manipulate.

Orange sticks, wooden cocktail sticks, scalpels, tweezers, probes and any other small modelling tools, dipped in water or acetone, are all useful for modelling – the more you have on hand the better.

Left: *On a figurine, the parts most prone to damage – some may even be missing – are the extremities. This harlequin is a valuable Meissen piece.*

Cup handle

Research the missing cup handle as discussed on p. 37, then draw it out on a piece of card. Make your drawing lifesize so that you can use it as a template. Hold your drawing against the cup and check that it looks right.

Make up some stiff epoxy-resin filler (see pp. 30-1) and leave it for about an hour, then roll it thin. If it does not roll out well, leave it for another half an hour or hour and repeat. Place the roll on your template, bend it to the correct shape and cut it to size. Make sure that your core of putty is thinner than the finished handle, then leave it until it is nearly dry.

Take this cup handle core and bond it on to the cup with some fresh epoxy-resin adhesive, with a little filling powder added. Stand the cup in a sand or salt box, and support the cup handle core with plastic modelling clay.

Once the core is firmly set, build up the handle with more putty and add any necessary embellishments.

Abrade and finish as described on pp. 34-5.

If you have to replace a cup handle, make sure that the style is in keeping with the rest of the cup – this may require research.

Modelling a cup handle

1 Draw out the handle on a piece of card.

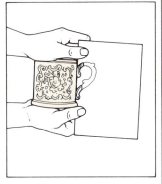

2 Check that the shape looks right against the cup.

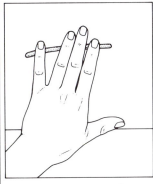

3 Roll out a thin core of epoxy-resin putty.

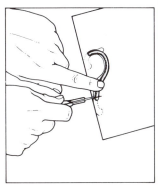

4 Bend it around the template; cut off the excess.

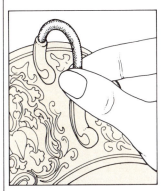

5 Bond the core to the cup with epoxy resin.

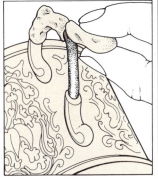

6 When the glue is dry, continue modelling on the cup.

Flowers

Use partly hardened epoxy-resin putty to make flowers, petals, leaves and so on, and put a little filling powder on your workboard or tile to prevent the putty from sticking.

Petals and leaves

For missing petals and leaves, roll or press a pellet of putty to the required thickness and cut it to shape using a scalpel dipped in acetone. Scrape a little adhesive on to the broken china and carefully transfer your petal or leaf. Support it with plastic modelling clay. If necessary, carry on modelling once it is attached to the piece, then leave it to dry. Finish as described on pp. 34-5.

Whole flowers

There will probably be unbroken flowers on your ornament and you can copy from these as you model. Examine them carefully to see how they were made. The more closely you copy the methods of the original modeller, the better match your own flowers will be.

Simple flowers on china were often made in one piece, and consist of four or five petals, sometimes with a slightly raised centre.

With your fingers, make a small ball of putty and shape it into a cone – the pointed end will be the stem of your flower. Hold the stem in one hand, and, with a

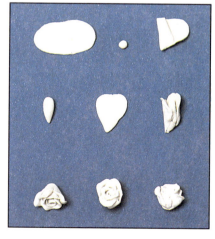

Leave the modelling material until it is firm enough to be pressed out very thin and will hold its shape without drooping.

round stick, make a hole down the centre of the wide end of the cone. With a sharp stick or scalpel dipped in acetone, indent or cut away the edges to make the required number of petals. If you need a raised centre, add a small 'dome' of putty. Leave it to dry and finish as described on pp. 34-5.

Roses are easier to make than they look. Flatten an oval of putty into an elongated shape, and curl it round a tiny ball for the centre. Flatten petals into fan shapes and place them alternately round the folded centre, so that they stand slightly higher than it. Tease the petals outwards into naturalistic shapes with your fingers or modelling tool, then gently roll and squeeze the base of the flower into a stem. Leave it to dry and finish as described on pp. 34-5.

Modelling replacements for missing flowers is very satisfying and not as difficult as it looks.

Hands

China figures with missing hands or fingers present the restorer with the most difficult job he is likely to undertake. Nevertheless, with a little perseverance, and practice, excellent results can be achieved. The best way to practise is to make hands in plastic modelling clay.

Look carefully at the figurine. Can you visualize a natural position for the hand? It is dependent on the posture of the whole figure, especially the arm. It may help to try out different hand positions *in situ* using plastic modelling clay. Perhaps the hand is holding something? If you cannot find an exact copy in a book, study as many similar figurines as possible; china figures are usually very stylized and themes and postures are repeated endlessly.

When you have decided on the positioning of the hand and fingers, study the style. It would be quite out of keeping to model a beautiful hand showing every knuckle and fingernail on a rough Staffordshire figure, for example. The intact hand is the most valuable guide for this. Next, consider the size. As you model, keep checking the other hand, making sure the one you are working on is the same size, not only in length and width, but in thickness. A pair of dividers or callipers can be a great help here. Note that a hand is just a little smaller than a face.

When you model replacement hands, make sure that they fit the style of the piece; they may be naturalistic or stylized.

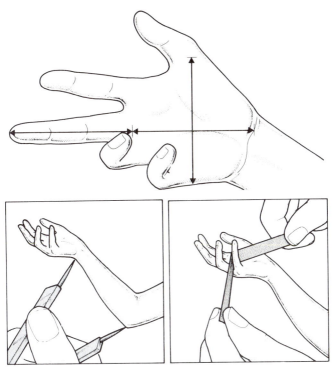

Note the proportions of your own hand, and use callipers to check the length of a modelled arm, for example. Use a thin strip of glasspaper to rub down between fingers.

Refer constantly to your own hand. If it is awkward to put your hand in the position of your modelled hand, then adjust your modelling. Study your own hand, each finger has three sections, and the tip of each is turned up (this is often exaggerated on china figures). See how the thumb is placed in relation to the fingers. The length of the longest finger is about the length of the palm, which is also the width of the palm, including the thumb (see above).

Always dip your tools, probes, scalpels and so on in water or acetone as you model. This will stop them sticking to the putty and pulling it out of shape.

When the hand is roughly correct but still pliable, bond it on to the arm with slow-setting epoxy resin, then make any minor adjustments. Support as described on pp. 14-15. When the hand is dry, carefully abrade it with files and abrasive papers, then add more putty, modelling as necessary. Make sure that the join is smooth with no filler overlapping.

Project 6: Art deco clowns

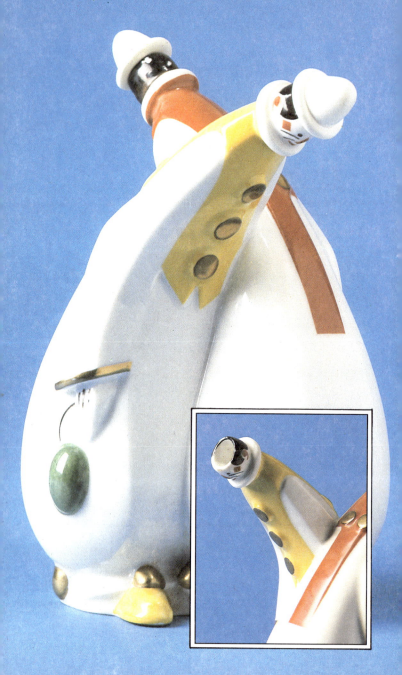

Making moulds

Although, as we have seen (pp. 36-43), modelling missing parts is not as difficult as first impressions might suggest, if you have an exact replica of a missing part, you will save a lot of time by making a mould. This is quite a common occurrence. You might, for example, have a double-handled vase, with one handle missing. In this case, make a mould of the handle you have and use it to produce an exact copy. Even if both handles are missing, you will still save time by modelling only the first and making a mould for the second.

The photograph illustrates this problem. These amusing art deco clowns were probably made to hold oil and vinegar. A photograph showed that their original tops were conical hats with corks embedded in them. Both tops are missing, but it will only be necessary to model one, and then construct a mould to make a copy.

For the mould, you will need some liquid latex rubber, which can be obtained from art or hardware shops where it is often sold as carpet or fabric adhesive. Briefly, the outside of the modelled hat is covered in latex which forms the mould. This is then removed and a liquid filler poured in. The most suitable liquid filler to use is liquid epoxy resin, but this is not always easy to obtain. You can, however, use ordinary epoxy resin if you heat it carefully first. This, when it has solidified, will give you a replica of the first hat.

You will also need a handful of sawdust, cotton-wool buds (Q-tip swabs), and, finally, an ordinary domestic oven.

A word of warning about latex: it can sometimes lift gilding off, so if you want to use this method on a gilded piece, test a tiny area first.

Modelling the first hat

Find two suitably sized corks. Model a hollow hat using an epoxy-resin putty (see pp. 30-1 and 37) and check that half the cork will fit inside.

When the first hat is modelled to your satisfaction, wash it to remove any dirt, grease and loose filling powder, and leave it to dry.

Left: *The most efficient method of replacing these clowns' hats is to model the first, make a rubber latex mould of it, then use this to make an exact replica.*

Moulding the second hat

Pour some liquid latex on to a saucer and dab it on the outside of the hat to the edge of the rim with a cotton-wool bud. This first coat of latex is the most important. Latex is very delicate, so do not touch or disturb it in any way. You will need three coats of latex, and should leave each to dry before applying the next.

Finally, to ensure that the mould is strong and fairly rigid, mix some sawdust with more latex and 'pat' it on with your fingers. Leave that until it is dry, then carefully remove the mould.

To make a liquid filler, mix some slow-setting epoxy resin and transfer it to a small, preferably disposable, container. Mix in some titanium dioxide to give it colour, then stir it thoroughly. Leave it for about 15 minutes to give the mixture time to settle, then place the container in the oven at a low temperature (about 120°C, 250°F). Check it every few minutes, because the resin only remains liquid for a few minutes, after which it hardens, so it is easy to leave it too long. If you do, discard the resin and begin again.

After about 10 minutes, the resin will have liquefied. Take it out of the oven (do not forget that the container will be hot, so use a tea towel/pot holder), invert the mould – a sandbox is ideal for holding it steady – and slowly pour the filler into the mould. So that you can embed the cork in the clown's hat, only half-fill the mould with resin and leave it for 24 hours to dry. Then make up some more liquid filler, place the cork in the centre, and fill around it to the brim. Leave this to dry for 24 hours, then remove the mould. The new hat will not be perfect, so abrade and fill it as described on pp. 34-5. Finally the hats can be painted (see pp. 48-59).

Leave the liquid epoxy resin to harden for at least 24 hours before you remove it from the mould.

Making a latex mould

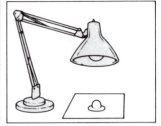

1 Dab latex on to model with a cotton-wool bud.

2 Speed drying under the heat of an angle-poise lamp.

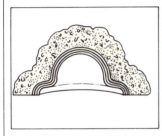

3 Use three layers of latex; mix sawdust with the third.

4 Fill the mould with liquid epoxy resin.

Two-part moulds

If you need a mould of something like a whole head, or a complete handle, you might find it impossible to remove the mould without distorting or breaking it. In this case, you can make a two-part mould. With a head, for example, make one mould for the face, and one for the back of the head.

Before making the face-side mould, press some plastic modelling clay over the surface of the back of the head, to act as a barrier against the first mould and to define its edge. Make one or two indentations on the clay, where it meets the first mould, to help you align the two half-moulds. Make the first half-mould as if it were a one-piece mould and leave it to set. When it has set, remove the modelling clay. Smear some washing-up (dishwashing) liquid or petroleum jelly around the edge of the set latex – this acts as a releasing agent when you need to separate the half-moulds. Now make the second mould, and when this has set, remove both. Join them together with a thin coat of latex, and proceed as for one-piece moulds.

Project 7: Eagle figure

Painting techniques

Earlier (pp. 28-35), coloured filler was used to fill in a chip in a vase. Coloured filler is an easy and effective way of making breaks and chips more acceptable to the eye; but they are never invisible. If you want to achieve an invisible or near invisible repair, it is necessary to paint.

Painting well on ceramics can be difficult and time-consuming although the results can be spectacular on many pieces of decorated and ornamental china. Such results are well within the capabilities of the amateur, given practice and the right methods and materials, though of course some pieces are by their nature more difficult to repair invisibly than others.

At first sight, this broken figure of an eagle may look like a daunting repair for an amateur to undertake. All the techniques involved in the reconstruction of the figure, however, have been discussed already in relation to earlier projects; here, they are all brought together and can be adapted to any other figure.

Whatever paints, pigments or glaze mediums you use, the painting technique is the same. The background colour (often, as here, white or nearly white) is applied first, followed by the decorative shades. Look closely at the eagle to determine the order in which the colours were originally applied; if you are able to copy this process, your repair and restoration will be more authentic.

Left: *Do not be tempted to save time by filling in and retouching a previous repair. As with this eagle, first dismantle and thoroughly clean each piece, then reconstruct the figure.*

Reconstructing the eagle

Remove every particle of glue, old filling material and paint, and clean each piece of the eagle carefully (as described on pp. 18-19), then wash, rinse, and leave them to dry.

Reconstruct the eagle one piece at a time with slow-setting epoxy resin. Each added piece must be left to dry, strapped and supported in a way which is appropriate to it, before the next is joined on (see pp. 14-15). As a general rule, on ornamental figures, do not be tempted to try bonding more than one piece at a time.

Filling and modelling

Use made-up or ready-made white epoxy-resin putty to fill in chips, and to model the missing flowers and legs (see pp. 30-1, and 36-43). All the filled surfaces, especially the joins, must be perfectly smooth to the touch; if they are not, the base coats of paint will highlight, rather than mask, the discrepancies (see pp. 34-5).

Filling in joins

However well you have bonded together two pieces of china, there will be, at least, a hairline crack. For an

To achieve an invisible restoration, all the joins and cracks must be filled in and rubbed down level with the surface.

Filling in joins

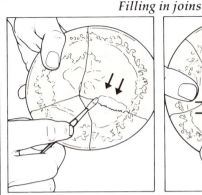 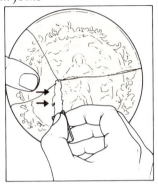

1 *Fill joins from the lower side to the higher.*

2 *Rub down from the higher side to the lower.*

invisible repair even these cracks must be filled and smoothed before you start painting. One side of the join will probably be a fraction higher than the other, so run a scalpel across the join to detect which. Sometimes, the alignment will change along the crack, from one side to the other.

Make up some thin putty as described on pp. 30-1, using less filling powder than for modelling or filling in chips, and fill the join from the *lower* side to the *higher*. Be as neat as you can and try not to overlap far on to the 'higher' side. When it has dried, rub down from the *higher* side to the *lower* in separate strokes. The filler should feather off on the lower side and leave a join that you cannot feel with your fingers. Repeat the process as many times as necessary.

Finish with a fine surface filler, or if you have difficulty obtaining that, make up your own (see p. 10) and apply this to the required area. Rub down the final thin filler with flour paper, once again working from the higher side to the lower.

Keep some of your used pieces of flour paper. They are useful to give an extra fine polish on your work; alternatively, buy the finest grade (1200) of silicon carbide wet and dry paper.

When the filling in and rubbing down have been completed, take your scalpel and scrape off any superfluous bits of filler on the piece. Wash the eagle thoroughly to remove any loose filling powder, dirt and grease, and leave it until it is bone dry.

It is now ready to be painted.

Pigments and paints

In project 4 (pp. 28-35), we saw how dry ground artist's pigments can be used to colour filler. These pigments can also be used as a base for your paints. Buy them in the smallest quantities you can, as a little tends to go a long way.

Pigments have to be mixed into a glaze or varnish medium (see pp. 54-5), so that they can be applied by brush. Some pigments disperse better than others. As a convenient alternative, small pots of ready-mixed enamel paints are widely available in model shops, toy shops and department stores. Initially, they are cheaper

Metallic colours see pp. 12-13 and 68-9.

White
You will already have titanium dioxide, which is essential for whitening filler. Buy this pigment in larger quantities, unless you are using ready-made paints.

Black
The densest is the best; this is usually called *lamp black*.

Blues
Ultramarine: a warm blue with a slight red hue.

Monastral, or astral blue: a cool blue tending towards green.

Indigo: a dark blue with a violet tone.

Greens
Monastral, or astral green: a rich green, tending towards blue.

Oxide of chrome: a lighter, more yellow green.

than buying a full range of powder pigments, but more expensive in the long run and less versatile.

In some art or craft shops, you may find ranges of enamel-type paints specially designed for painting on china or glass. If you buy ready-made paints, make sure you purchase the clear varnish or glaze, and plenty of the thinners which are sold with them.

Colours

The names of the same colours can vary according to the manufacturer, so if you are in any doubt, take this colour chart to the shop and check them.

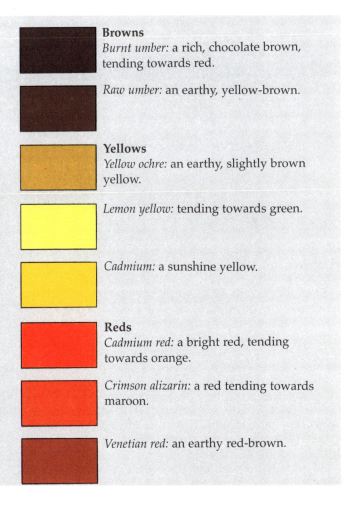

Browns
Burnt umber: a rich, chocolate brown, tending towards red.

Raw umber: an earthy, yellow-brown.

Yellows
Yellow ochre: an earthy, slightly brown yellow.

Lemon yellow: tending towards green.

Cadmium: a sunshine yellow.

Reds
Cadmium red: a bright red, tending towards orange.

Crimson alizarin: a red tending towards maroon.

Venetian red: an earthy red-brown.

Varnishes and glaze mediums

If you use powder pigments, you must also buy a clear glaze or varnish medium and the appropriate thinning agent. Art and craft shops sell various types of varnishes, some of which are suitable for china restoration, so check the labels or instruction leaflets. Also, the clear varnish sold with the ready-made enamel-type paints can be bought separately and mixed with artist's powder pigments.

Most professional restorers use one, or both, of two types of glazes, which are not generally available. However, some art or craft shops do sell (or may order) them. If you can buy these, do so, as they are superior in various ways to most other varnishes.

The first type of glaze (a urea formaldehyde resin) sets with the addition of a catalyst, and is then workable for 24 hours if you keep it in an airtight bottle, or for two days or more if kept in a refrigerator.

The second type is stoving enamel glaze. For this you need a (preferably electric) oven or plate warmer. After each application the piece is placed in the oven for an hour at a very low temperature (90-120°C, 200-250°F). Once removed from the oven and left to cool, the glaze is very tough and the next stage of painting can be overlaid immediately, unlike all the other varnishes which often need up to 24 hours to harden. Stoving enamel glaze is probably the hardest and most yellow-resistant varnish available. Most pieces can be treated with stoving enamel but exercise discretion and do not put very delicate or old pieces in an oven. Always remove any metal rims, bases and so on before stoving any piece.

The setting time of all varnishes (except the stoving type) can be speeded up if you place the piece in a warm environment, such as the top of a radiator, or under an angle-poise lamp. Do not be tempted to add more coats of paint until the one underneath has set to its maximum hardness.

When you buy them, varnishes are usually thicker than you will need for china restoration. It is a good idea to decant some into a small jar and add thinning agent; the amount will depend on the varnish (experience will teach you the correct proportion), and work with this thinned varnish.

Always keep a separate small glass jar of thinners for cleaning brushes, tiles and so on.

Painting techniques

1 Mix paints and pigments in a metal dipper.

2 Transfer thinners and varnishes with a dropper.

3 Use finest quality sable brushes for painting.

4 Cure stoving enamels in an oven.

Painting

Your paintbrushes should be finest quality sable, and numbers 00 and 2 are probably the most useful to begin with. Look after your brushes, clean them in whatever thinning agent you are using before the paint on the brush dries out. Do not use your sable brushes to mix pigments – they will quickly be ruined. Instead, use an old, larger, *clean* brush (about size 6).

The more tiny glass jars with lids you have the better. These are useful for keeping and decanting solvents, made-up paints, thinners and so on. Use an eye-dropper for transferring thinners and varnishes – never a brush, however clean you may think it is.

Small metal dippers for mixing up pigments or paints can be purchased from art shops. Clean them in thinners immediately after use. Metal bottle tops, small egg cups and so on can be used instead, in fact, any small clean receptacle, as long as it is not plastic. Use soft toilet paper or cotton rags dipped in thinners for cleaning up.

Base coats and background colours

Almost all pieces of china have a white background. If you look more closely, however, the white background is actually never pure white; observe this yourself by comparing a pure white tile with any piece of china. You must aim to match the background perfectly; this is sometimes the most difficult part of colour matching.

Applying base coats

Before you apply the background colour, paint a coat of pure white colour along the lines of the cracks, joins, and modelled parts to cover all the filler. Try not to overlap on to the original china by more than a fraction. A number 2 brush is usually appropriate. Apply the paint, which should be the consistency of thin cream, in one smooth stroke over each area, so there are no brushstrokes visible.

There will be a hard line at the edges of the paint where it meets the original china. You can feather this out by cleaning your brush and applying short angled strokes of pure glaze along the edge. Do this immediately before the paint starts to dry, which it will after only a minute or two, for all paints other than stoving enamels. Practise this feathering out technique on a black tile. Feathering out hard lines is important – the join will never become invisible if you don't do it.

After about 10 minutes, depending on the medium, apply a coat of clear glaze or varnish over the painted

After you have finished filling in and modelling, apply the first base coat; this should be pure white, followed by a tinted background colour.

area. Paint it as lightly and swiftly as possible, or the thinners in the glaze may disturb the painting underneath. If it does, try applying a slightly thicker glaze (that is, with less thinners).

When this first coat has thoroughly dried (or stoved if you are using a stoving glaze), examine the restoration so far. The paint will highlight any discrepancies, holes, ridges and imperfectly filled cracks and joins. Small blemishes may disappear with subsequent coats of paint, but you may well have to return to the filling in stage, using a fine surface filler, then rub that down and paint on another coat of white paint and glaze. To obliterate the joins completely, you may need several coats of white paint, each covered with a coat of glaze. To avoid a lumpy look and feel, carefully abrade with the finest flour paper or wet and dry you have, after each coat of glaze or varnish. Rub down from the centre of the paint to the outside. If you work from the outside inwards, you may lift off the paint.

Colour matching the background

When all the joins are invisible, you are ready to paint on the background colour. This is white, with minute quantities of colour. Take a number of pieces of china, both ornamental and domestic, and study their background colours. Almost invariably you will find they are either a 'cool' tone, tending towards blue, or a 'warm' tone tending towards yellow. Most oriental and hard-paste chinas are cool, while softer paste ceramics tend to be warm. For cool tones, with your white, mix in tiny amounts of both ultramarine and yellow ochre. For warm tones, mix in a few grains of burnt umber and lemon yellow. Occasionally, you may need to add traces of other colours; the exact amounts, of course, vary from piece to piece.

In a dipper, put some white, plus a little glaze and thinners to make the consistency of thin cream, and adjust it to the correct background colour. Add drops of thinners occasionally with an eye-dropper, so that the paint does not dry out. Test your colour matching by dabbing a little on an original part of the china. Clean it off with thinners immediately afterwards.

Apply the background colour in the same way as you did the white base coats, finishing with a coat of glaze. If the match is not perfect, leave it to dry, rub it down lightly and try again.

Decoration: transparent and semi-transparent colours

A transparent colour is pure colour, semi-transparent colours contain some white. Look closely at your piece. On the eagle, there are a number of bright colours; a yellow beak, green foliage, purple flowers, and black, grey and brown feathers. There are also light washes of colour underneath some of the bright colours. In fact, there are fewer colours than appearance suggests. The grey, for example, is a watery black and the light yellow is the same as the yellow on the beak but less dense.

For light washes, put some glaze medium into your dipper or, if you need only a small amount of paint, on your tile. Then add pigments or paints, until you achieve the correct tint. Add thinners as necessary. These washes are often semi-transparent colours and need some white in their composition.

Apply the paint by flowing it on to the china rather than in neat brushstrokes. Test on a nearby, but unrestored, part for colour match. Once painted, protect the coat with a layer of clear varnish.

The denser, bright colours, are mostly pure colour with little glaze added, or, if you are using ready-made paints, no glaze at all. Adding a tiny bit of raw umber is often the best way to darken a colour.

Remember that you are working over a delicate background colour. If you make a mistake in decorat-

Typical crazing on a Staffordshire figure. With practice, it is possible to paint lines thinly enough to simulate crazing.

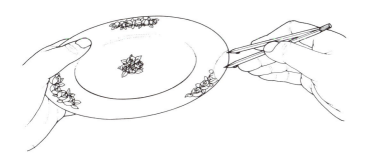

If you have a repeated pattern, round the edge of a plate, for example, use callipers to measure distances.

ing, cleaning it off with thinners can disturb the base coats. If this happens, leave it to dry, rub down and apply more base coats. However, if you have painted a thin line too thickly, you can take a clean brush, barely dampened in thinners, and run it along the edge of the line. This will thin and neaten the line without disturbing the paint underneath. Do this as soon as possible, before the paint dries too much.

To finish, cover all your work in a final coat of clear varnish or glaze medium.

If the decoration stands too proud of the surface, after applying the final coat of varnish and letting it dry, lightly rub down the surface with your finest abrasive paper, then finish off with more clear varnish. This process can be repeated again if necessary.

Hints on painting

Difficult decoration can be pencilled in lightly on the area to be painted with a hard pencil.

For a **matt finish**, add some talcum powder to the glaze medium. The more you add, the less glossy will be the finish.

Some **crazing** on china can be effectively imitated by very thin lines of paint (often raw umber and a touch of white, in a suitably thinned medium).

On **blue and white ceramics**, use ultramarine and indigo, *never* astral blue for the blue.

Flesh colour is semi-transparent, that is composed of glaze medium, white and thinners, plus some yellow ochre and cadmium red. If there is a 'flush' of transparent colour over this semi-transparent one, use the same formula, but without the white.

Project 8: Worcester jug

Advanced painting and gilding

This is the most ambitious project so far. Not only is this Worcester jug badly damaged with large missing pieces, it also has flat areas of paint with little decoration. The less top decoration there is on a piece, the harder it is to achieve an invisible restoration.

As before, however, you do not need knowledge of any new techniques in order to repair the jug. First of all, the old restoration has to be stripped down and the pieces cleaned and rebonded. There are large areas missing on the jug, both around the base and the neck. Here, too, the tasks are more complex than before, but they build on the techniques learned in previous projects. As before, all the joins have to be filled in and rubbed down so that they are perfectly flush with the original china.

Buying an airbrush

Although an acceptable finish can be obtained by hand painting, the only really effective way to make invisible restorations on pieces like this with either a plain background or a light wash is with an airbrush.

The airbrush is a pen-sized spray gun which leaves no brushstrokes, so is ideal for use on plain surfaces. It is also faster than painting background colours by hand. The stages involved in obliterating the cracks and painting the background colours are, however, the same as if you were hand painting, and the coats of varnish are applied in the same way.

Good-quality airbrushes are expensive (cheap ones do not give good results), as is a good compressor. You can buy cans of air from art shops, but they do not last very long. Airbrushing requires a great deal of practice for the results to be satisfactory and airbrushes must be meticulously cleaned after *every* use. They are also tricky to use with the paints used in china restoration. For all these reasons, think very seriously before you buy an airbrush; if you have only one or two pieces of china to restore, it is not worth the investment.

Finally, the missing pieces of gilding on the jug have to be replaced.

Left: The top of the jug reconstructed but before filling; note the missing piece on the base. The quality of the final finish will depend on the quality of the earlier stages of bonding and filling in.

Preliminary stages

First of all, the old restoration must be stripped down in water, and/or paint stripper (see pp. 22-3) and cleaned thoroughly. When all the pieces are dry, bond the jug back together again, one piece at a time, using slow-setting epoxy resin, and leave it until the glue is dry.

Fill in the missing pieces around the neck of the jug using epoxy-resin filler as described on pp. 28-35. Use plastic modelling clay and clear adhesive tape to support the filler as you build it up. As before, underfill, rather than overfill, the chips, then add more filler if necessary. This may save you a great deal of tiresome rubbing down. Use a sandbox to support the jug while the filled-in pieces set and dry. Abrade them as described on pp. 34-5, taking special care not to damage the original china.

Repairing the base

A useful tip for replacing the large missing area on the base is, in effect, to make a mould (see pp. 44-7). Take a latex impression of the top of a good part of the base

To fill a large missing area, either model freehand or use the latex-impression method. Take care when you rub down around gilding – it is more delicate than other colours.

Replacing a large missing area

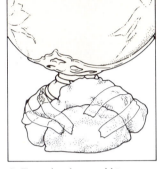

1 *Take a latex impression of a good area.*

2 *Transfer the mould to cover the missing area.*

3 *Invert, then pour in liquid epoxy resin.*

4 *When the resin is dry, remove the mould.*

but make it a little larger than the piece to be filled. When this is dry, transfer it to cover the missing area. Secure it well with clear adhesive tape and plastic modelling clay, then turn the jug over and carefully fill in the missing portion with liquid filler. Make sure that you do not disturb the latex mould. Leave it to dry, then remove the mould. You should find the top half of the missing piece neatly filled to the right shape.

As with project 7, before you start to paint, all the filled and missing pieces must be *perfectly* flush with the original china, and the joins and cracks tapered off imperceptibly. Your fingers are a better guide than your eyes for determining if there is any ridge between the filler and the china.

Painting

In many cases, hand painting gives a very good finish and you could achieve a reasonable finish on this jug using the techniques outlined for painting the eagle on pp. 56-9. There, little discrepancies in the background colour were hidden when the thicker and darker transparent colours were overlaid.

Hardest of all to paint is a plain white plate with no decoration. However good your feathering and colour-matching techniques, it is unlikely that you will be able to blend perfectly into the original, and you will probably end up overpainting more and more on to the china in an attempt to do so. Generally it is better not to paint such a piece, but simply to bond it together, leaving just a neat hairline crack (as in projects 2 and 3, pp. 20-7), and filling any little chips and holes with coloured filler (see project 4, pp. 28-35).

The Worcester jug has a plain background only on the inside of the top and underneath on the base. Nonetheless, the colours on the jug are all light washes which present the restorer with similar problems. The only really effective way of invisibly restoring pieces like these is with an airbrush.

Airbrushing is a complicated skill, but if you would like to try it, there are many books available which give more information than space permits here.

Airbrushing the jug

An airbrush leaves no brushstrokes, so the problem of plain surfaces can be overcome. It is also faster than painting background colours by hand.

The stages to be followed to obliterate cracks and to paint on the background colour with an airbrush are the same as if you were hand painting, so follow the directions outlined on pp. 50-1 and 56-7. Spray the white base coats on to the smoothed surface using small circular motions, and progress along the cracks as you do so. As before, in between coats of paint, spray on a coat of varnish.

Take extra care when you are rubbing down between coats when you use an airbrush. The film of both paint and glaze is so fine that you could lift a portion off.

When you paint the background colour, the best way to blend the colour into the background is to 'fade' it off slightly at the edges (see pp. 66-7). Make sure that you have practised this technique thoroughly before you start airbrushing any piece.

One problem in airbrushing is the danger of excessive overspraying on the original china. Masking off the surrounding area with masking tape can help.

Cover each coat of background colour with a coat of glaze, and – as with hand painting – finish with a coat of glaze.

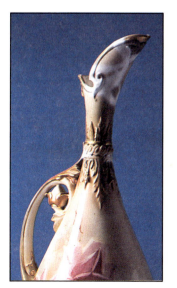

Left: *After reconstruction* (far left), *fill in all the missing areas with epoxy-resin putty* (centre), *carefully modelling the raised decoration. Finish with a fine surface filler, then paint or, if you are using an airbrush, spray on the first base coat, keeping the overspray to a minimum.*

Airbrushes and airbrushing

Briefly, an airbrush is fed by compressed air, which, when mixed with paint, emits a fine spray of colour through the nozzle at the front. Colour is mixed in a paint cup on the instrument. The breadth of spray can be finely adjusted.

The compressor should be able to deliver at least 25 p.s.i., preferably 40 p.s.i. Before spraying paint, always spray some thinners through the airbrush to clean it and check that there are no blockages in the nozzle parts. If there are, dismantle the nozzle and clean.

If you are using ground pigments, ensure that they are well dispersed in glaze medium and thinners before introducing them into the paint cup supplied with the airbrush. Otherwise, gritty bits of pigment will cause the spray to splutter and may even block the nozzle. For the same reason, add more thinners to the paint than you would for hand painting.

Controls for spraying vary according to the make of airbrush, though they all have a long needle which, when retracted by means of a lever, controls the breadth of spray.

With a white paint mixture in your paint cup, practise painting thin straight lines on a black tile. The nearer the airbrush is to the surface to be sprayed, the finer the lines with less overspray. However, the needle or retracting lever must be pulled back only a fraction or your fine line will turn into a puddle. Stir the paint mixture in the cup frequently.

If your fine lines keep speckling, there is either a tiny blockage in the nozzle, which you must clean or soak in thinners, or the paint itself is too thick and needs thinning down (simply add more thinners with an eye-dropper and stir with your mixing brush).

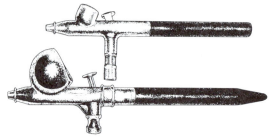

The type of airbrushes suitable for china restoration have nozzles which are easy to dismantle for cleaning.

The airbrush

1 Stir the paint in the cup to avoid separation.

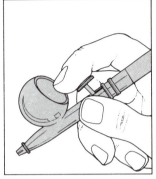

2 A lever, usually on top, controls the width of spray.

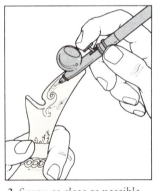

3 Spray as close as possible to avoid overspray.

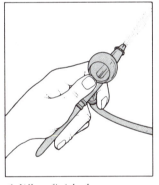

4 When finished, spray through clean thinners.

After you have gained some confidence in spraying thin lines, practise spraying thicker lines, using tiny circular motions, one circle overlapping the one before as you spray along the tile. Next, practise 'fading off', by pulling the spray across and up from the tile. This technique is used for blending in the background colour to the surrounding china, and for washes of colour that fade out.

Speckled effects can be achieved by retracting the needle, reducing the pressure, and/or using a thicker paint medium. Painting some types of decoration can also be achieved with a good airbrush.

Finally, if you are using an airbrush, *always* work in a well-ventilated room, and wear a vapour mask.

Gilding

Always apply gold decoration last, and make sure before you begin that all other painting is finished and completely dry. Highly mirrored gold is impossible to reproduce well. Fortunately, this is only found on modern pieces. Antique gold is duller, although even the finest quality gold leaf cannot perfectly match some finishes.

Many art shops sell **ready-made gold** and silver preparations. These are simple to use and it is worth buying as many different shades as possible, because gold decoration is so often found on china. After painting them on, burnish with a soft cloth.

Finely ground **bronze powders** give a gold with a slightly better finish than ready-mixed paints, and they are more versatile. Again, buy as many shades as you can. Mix them together dry, then, when the required shade has been reached, add a few drops of glaze medium (too much glaze tends to give a duller finish) to bind them together, plus a little thinner if necessary. Apply them with a paintbrush. Do not apply a coat of clear glaze over the top, as it will dull the shine, just burnish with a soft cloth. These preparations can, of course, be mixed together and pigments and paints added.

For large areas of bright gold, **gold leaf** can give the best results. Gold leaf is difficult to apply, and sometimes the results are disappointing. It is expensive as it

An effective way of using bronze powders for an area like the base of the jug is to sprinkle them on to a tacky coat of glaze. When the varnish is dry, wash the piece – the 'gold' will be left adhering to the glaze underneath. Burnish it when the piece is dry.

Applying gold leaf

1 With a very sharp scalpel, cut a square of gold leaf.

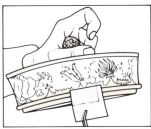

2 Transfer the leaf and its tissue backing to the piece.

3 Gently rub the tissue backing with your fingers.

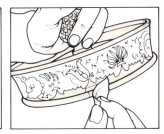

4 Peel off the tissue; burnish when the varnish is dry.

comes in books of 25 leaves. There are cheaper imitation gold leaves available, which on some pieces are just as good. There are various shades available, so if you want to try it, take the piece of china to your supplier (not all art shops sell it) and find the closest match. For china restoring purposes, *transfer gold leaf* is the most convenient form to use.

Gold leaf application is illustrated above. Apply a thin even coat of varnish with a little yellow pigment or paint to the area of china to be gilded. Wait until the varnish is tacky (15-30 mins) before applying the leaf.

When the varnish has dried, burnish with an agate gold leaf burnisher, or a very hard smooth rounded gemstone (for example in a ring). More than one coat of gold leaf may be needed.

Lustre finishes usually have a copper base. Pigments and paints can be added to them to achieve different lustrous shades and effects. Many lustre effects consist mainly of pigments with just a small amount of copper added. Unfortunately, however, it is impossible to match some of these effects well.

Project 9: Ceramic tiles

In this section, we will examine the techniques involved in restoring old ceramic tiles. They also apply to other soft-bodied ceramics, such as pottery, earthenware and plaster figures.

Cleaning and bonding

Be more careful than usual when you clean soft-bodied ceramics. Unglazed ceramic crumbles and flakes quite easily when subjected to a scalpel or even medium-grade abrasive papers. Also, the material can be so porous that it soaks up water like a sponge. Although it will dry out again, if the edge of the break is very grimy, the water may carry the dirt underneath the glaze and leave a stain. For this reason, never use the hydrogen-peroxide method of stain removal (pp. 18-19). Similarly, prolonged soaking in water softener and biological detergent is not recommended. Soapy water can be used to clean many types of soft ceramics, but if you are in any doubt, just de-grease and try to remove stains by using the various solvents like acetone. Test them on a small piece first.

Soft pottery is so porous that bonding with epoxy resins is not very effective, because much of the adhesive soaks into the pottery. Use PVA (yellow) adhesive, which is usually sold as wood glue, instead.

It is unlikely that you will be able to achieve the sort of hairline join on soft pottery possible on china because it crumbles so easily, and flakes and chips of pottery will probably have broken off when it was originally damaged. Once you have bonded a piece, you should fill the imperfect joins.

Filling in soft-bodied ceramics

The smooth, hard, china-like finish of epoxy-resin filler is not appropriate to unglazed soft-bodied ceramics, which are more easily damaged when you come to sanding down. Also the texture is quite different. You should use a filler which is softer when set, and gives a matt, coarser finish – the types sold for filling in small cracks and holes in walls and plaster are ideal. You can also add dry artist's pigments to them if you want coloured filler; this often looks very effective on pottery.

Left: *These typical Victorian tiles are made of a soft, porous ceramic with a glaze on the top surface.*

Filling in tiles

Tiles, though composed of soft pottery, have a tough glaze on the surface, so filling in with epoxy-resin filler is quite suitable. Fill in and rub down as described on pp.30-5. To fill a missing corner make a wall of small toy interlocking bricks or use plastic modelling clay or other straight-sided objects to support the filler.

Put the tile and wall on a disposable piece of card in case the filler runs underneath. Smear petroleum jelly on and under the wall and tile; this acts as a releasing agent when the liquid filler has dried. To reduce run-off, either place weights on the wall, or attempt to seal around it with plastic modelling clay. Underfill slightly, rather than overfill. When it has dried, this filler is very hard, and it is very time-consuming to rub it down even if you have only slightly overfilled.

When the filler is dry, remove the wall, then fill in and rub down as described on pp. 34-5.

Painting

Paint the tile as described on pp. 56-9. Use several white base coats, and then apply the background colour. Use a coat of glaze medium over each, and lightly rub down all the coats except the last one.

Hand paint the decoration, using either ground pigments in a glaze medium or ready-bought paints, and finish with a coat of glaze.

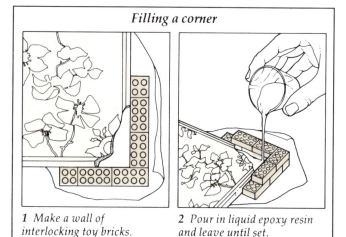

Filling a corner

1 Make a wall of interlocking toy bricks.

2 Pour in liquid epoxy resin and leave until set.

Rubbing down is often easier on tiles because the surface is flat, unlike vases, figurines and so on. For a full restoration, the base coats, background colours and decoration should be applied as for china.

Simple breaks

This tile is broken in half. As we have seen, epoxy resin is not suitable for bonding soft pottery, so here we will use PVA adhesive (wood glue). First, make a thin solution of PVA by adding water, and then paint it on to both sides of the break with an old clean paintbrush. It will be soaked up immediately, but it will form a barrier so that when you apply neat PVA (to *both* sides of the join), it will work effectively.

Clear adhesive tape does not stick well to unglazed surfaces, so to support the tile while the glue dries (about 24 hours), bring the two halves together on as

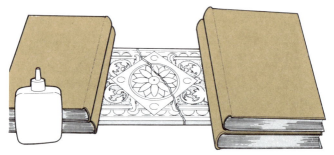

Use woodworking glue to bond tiles and support the join between two heavy books until the adhesive is dry.

A partial restoration can often give good, quick results. Use coloured filler, and paint the decoration directly on to it.

Soft-bodied ceramics can be unglazed, partly glazed or glazed. Although the methods of restoration are the same, the materials used must vary accordingly.

level a surface as possible. If one side of the join is slightly higher than the other, place pieces of plastic modelling clay underneath the lower half of the tile to raise it up slightly. Adjust it in this way until the join is level. You should now put some weight on either side of the tile – heavy books are ideal. Do not use a tourniquet on broken tiles; it tends to make the joins misalign.

Painting

As we have seen, often the most difficult aspect of painting a piece is to match the background colour satisfactorily. If you wish, quite acceptable and fast results can be achieved by omitting this stage and simply painting on the decoration once the piece has been bonded and filled.

Obliterate the crack as best you can by filling it with a white epoxy filler (see pp. 30-1), rub it down, and then disguise it with the painted decoration.

If your tile is to be used in a fireplace, this method is particularly good, because painting may deteriorate if you light a fire under it, and the background may yellow far faster than the decoration.

When you paint unglazed ceramics, use powder pigments in preference to ready-bought enamel paints. Use a smaller amount of glaze medium, and if necessary add a matting agent (see p. 59).

A word of warning: do not use stoving enamels with PVA adhesive.

Acknowledgements

Swallow Books gratefully acknowledge the assistance given to them in the production of *Repairing Old China and Ceramic Tiles* by the following people and organizations. We apologize to anyone we may have omitted to mention.

Photographs: Jon Bouchier 1, 6, 7, 8, 10, 11, 13, 16, 17, 20, 24, 27, 28, 33, 40, 44, 46, 48, 49, 50, 56, 58, 60, 62, 64, 65, 68, 70, 73, 74; The Bridgeman Art Library 38; Michael Holford 36, 41, 42; Elizabeth Whiting and Associates 4, 75 – photographer Ann Kelley.

Restoration on pages 16, 17, 20, 24, 27, 28, 33, 44, 46, 48, 49, 50, 56, 58, 60, 62, 64, 65, 68, 70, 74 by Jeff Oliver.

Illustrations: Hussein Hussein 74; Aziz Khan 30, 43; Coral Mula 14, 18, 33, 34, 35, 39, 47, 51, 59, 63, 69; Stuart Perry 22, 67, 72; Rob Shone 27, 55, 68.